D1611804

WHY ARE YOUR PAPERS IN ORDER?

Other Avon Books by
S. Gross

AN ELEPHANT IS SOFT AND MUSHY
I AM BLIND AND MY DOG IS DEAD

WHY ARE ___
YOUR PAPERS
IN ORDER?
CARTOONS FOR 1984

EDITED AND
FOREWORD BY___
___ S. GROSS

AVON
PUBLISHERS OF BARD, CAMELOT, DISCUS AND FLARE BOOKS

WHY ARE YOUR PAPERS IN ORDER? is an original
publication of Avon Books. This work has never before
appeared in book form.

Further Copyright notices appear on the Acknowledgments
page and serve as an extension of this Copyright page.

AVON BOOKS
A division of
The Hearst Corporation
1790 Broadway
New York, New York 10019

First Avon Printing, November, 1983

AVON TRADEMARK REG. U.S. PAT. OFF. AND IN
OTHER COUNTRIES, MARCA REGISTRADA, HECHO EN
U.S.A.

Printed in the U.S.A.

DON 10 9 8 7 6 5 4 3 2 1

Acknowledgments

Of the 182 drawings in this collection, 31 appeared originally in *The New Yorker;* Copyright © 1948, 1957, 1967, 1970, 1973, 1974, 1975, 1976, 1977, 1978, 1979, 1980.

Pages 8-9 and 52-53: Cartoons from pages 11-13 and 52-53 of GROUP THERAPY by Lou Myers. Copyright © 1960, 1962, 1963, 1964, 1965 by Lou Myers. Reprinted by permission of Harper & Row, Publishers, Inc.

Page 18: © 1975 by Stuart Leeds, *The New York Times.*

Page 23, cartoon A: From: *Running A Muck* by John Caldwell © 1978, by permission of Writer's Digest Books.

The following are reprinted by permission of Tribune Company Syndicate, Inc.:
Page 29, cartoon A: Joseph Mirachi, September 1, 1978.
Page 36: Ed Fisher, October 7, 1976
Page 113, cartoon A: Brian Savage, March 31, 1979
Page 169: Mort Gerberg, March 2, 1976
Page 174: Ed Fisher, March 29, 1980

Page 49, cartoon A: Copyright *The Washington Post.* Michael Crawford, Monday, July 16, 1979.

Page 74, cartoon B: Reprinted by permission of The National Lampoon. Charles Rodriguez, 1975.

Pages 84-85: Reprinted by permission of *Mother Jones Magazine.* M.K. Brown.

Page 87 and Pages 146-147: Reproduced by Special Permission of PLAYBOY Magazine; Copyright © 1974 and © 1975 by *Playboy.* George Booth.

Foreword

Righteousness has never been one of my strong suits (pig-headedness and hanging up my clothes are), but it's difficult not to get sucked into extolling what is good and lamenting what is bad if you're going to write about 1984. After all, 1984 has become a buzz word (or buzz number if you want to nitpick), as a result, I have a temptation to comment on the problems we are experiencing in the world today. What's even worse is that I am perfectly willing to expound upon my solutions to these problems, but I have good news: I am going to resist doing it. Instead, I am going to write about cartoonists and the cartoons in this book.

The first thing you should know about cartoonists is that they have a tendency to be fiercely independent. I don't believe that they behave this way out of any sense of nobility, but rather out of a sense of perversity. To give you an illustration: If you were an editor and you told a group of cartoonists that you had an overabundance of desert island cartoons and that you never wanted to see another one, the next week you would be inundated with desert island gags. If by chance you bought a few (and as history has previously borne out, you most probably would), the cartoonists who sold you those ideas, instead of being grateful, would probably consider you a jerk.

Fortunately, we cartoonists are not too often inspired in the manner given in the example. Most of the time we get our ideas by circulating whatever creative juices are available to us at that moment. It may look like we are not doing anything, but by running our minds over things we know and have experienced as well as mulling over the things we feel strongly about, we might just come up with an idea. We repeat this process over and over, and eventually come up with enough ideas to make a presentation to show an editor.

As for the cartoons in this book, I've tried to pick out the ones I thought would most vigorously express the feelings of the artists; in other words, the result of all those hours of mulling. The majority of these cartoons are not political cartoons. They are the "gag" or "panel" cartoons, and the difference between them and political cartoons is that the primary purpose of these cartoons is to make people laugh. Their secondary purpose may be to make a political or social comment, but, at the time these ideas were conceived, I can pretty well assure you that going for the laugh came first.

With some of these cartoons, however, the laugh elicited may be a nervous one. With others, the reader might so disagree with what the cartoonist has produced as to be provoked to anger. While I don't particularly welcome such a reaction, I do prefer it to indifference, which to a cartoonist is about the most reprehensible thing that can happen to him professionally. I don't think you'll be indifferent to this book, and I hope you will enjoy it.

S. GROSS
May, 1983.

WHY ARE YOUR PAPERS IN ORDER?

"A special prosecutor was appointed today to investigate every
damn last one of us."

"Wake up, wake up, whoever you are! This is 1984!"

"It's been done."

"Stop!—He's our informant!"

"*Somebody bugged my office. Somebody cares!*"

"I don't agree with what you say, but for ten bucks I'll defend
to the death your right to say it."

"Oh, you press the button down.
The data goes 'round and around,
Whoa-ho-ho-ho-ho-ho
And it comes out here."

"Nothing for you except for some junk mail from Amnesty International."

"I love his fireside chats."

"*I see Elsie Littleton informed on her husband. Well it's about time.*"

"*Hi! I'm Big Brother, and I'm running for President in '84.*"

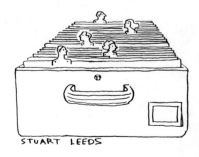

STUART LEEDS

WHAT THEY STILL BELIEVE IN

MATCH COLUMN A with COLUMN B

(A)

(B)

MANIFEST DESTINY

PILTDOWN MAN

CAPITALISM

COMMON SENSE

ORGONE BOXES

R. Chast

Bernard Schoenbaum.

"I don't know how to interpret this. The polygraph says he's telling the truth but he insists he's lying."

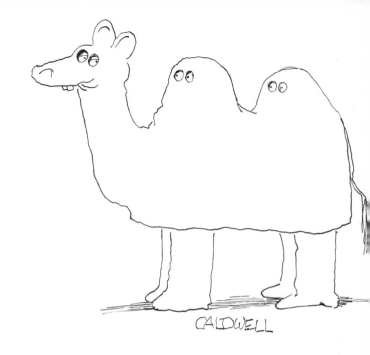

"*You know that you are viewing me. Are you absolutely sure?*
Can it be instead, that I am the viewer and you, the viewee?"

"If I hear one more 'I told you so' from that Orwell chap I'm going to punch him in the nose!"

"Think of it, Natasha, all those other police states out there to undermine."

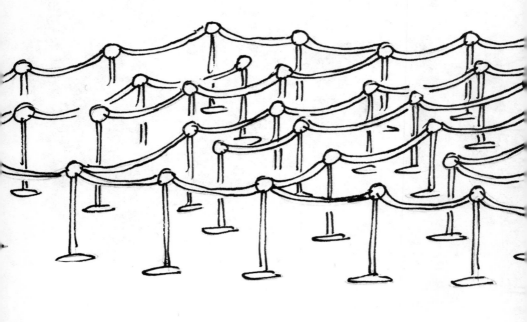

"Did you know you're bugged? There's a little mike in your sideburn."

ENTER
THE
SYSTEM
HERE

S. GROSS

VAST IMPROVEMENTS

From "cheese" to CHEASE

From "flute" to FLOOT

From "cookie" to CUKY

R. Chast

"Are you uninformed or apathetic?" "I don't know and I don't care."

BOOTH

S.GROSS

"Congratulations! You're having a boy!"

"We're here from Amnesty International."

"The usual."

"Oh yeah! According to my voice-stress analyzer, you're lying!"

BY 1984, FEMALE PRIESTS AND MALE NUNS HAD BECOME ALMOST AS COMMONPLACE AS TENNIS WHITES HAD BECOME PASSÉ.

"Simon says, 'Go to work, have a few martinis, come home, have a drink, eat, watch some TV, and go to sleep.'"

"And there's been a lot of loose talk lately about so-called
'disappearances.'"

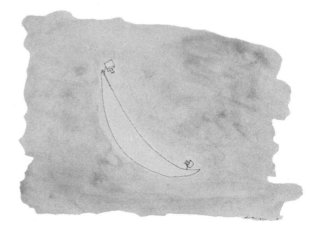

"Why is that man laughing?"

"Mea Culpa, I'd like you to meet J'Accuse."

SCENIC
AREA

Front row (left to right): one, two, three, four, five, six, seven, eight, nine. Standing: ten, eleven, twelve, thirteen, fourteen, fifteen, sixteen, seventeen. Not present: eighteen.

"I have to take one three times a day to curb my insatiable appetite for power."

"One good thing—it's safe to walk the streets again."

"We're in luck. He's in!"

*"Of course I'll marry you...just as soon as I shake this
surveillance."*

*"Do you get the feeling that the Ministry of Information is not
telling us everything?"*

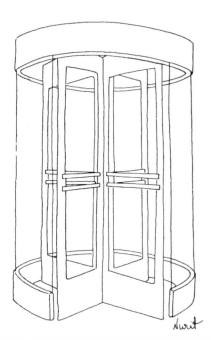

S. GROSS

"Which one did you say was the figurehead?" Or are they all figureheads?"

"Grayson is a liberal in social matters, a conservative in
economic matters, and a homicidal psychopath in political
matters."

"Here's a tour you may enjoy...eleven police states in fourteen days."

"…except, of course, where noted (*)."

"Come to think of it, I don't ever remember hearing it cuckoo."

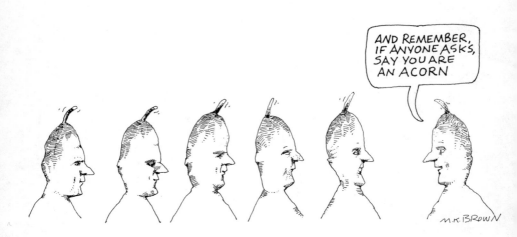

"One vote, one man."

"I lie down with lambs because I can bully them."

"The way I look at it, if we don't do it, someone else will."

2.

3.

④.

⑤.

ZIEGLER

"...*the move has been made and seconded.*"

"*We have to be forthright with the public. We have to have their confidence. We have to convince them we're working for the common good. Then we can invade their privacy.*"

"Mr. Kagan isn't with us anymore. He's been vaporized."

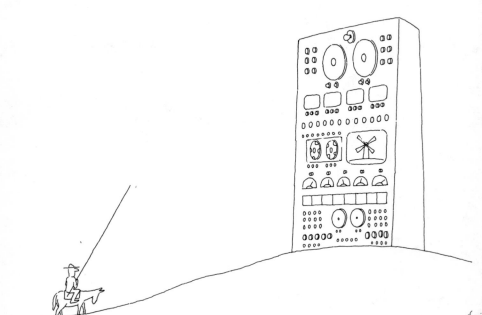

"*If elected, I promise that people won't be violently beaten about the head and chest area...so much.*"

"To the Housing Authority, Port Authority, Tunnel Authority, Transit Authority, Bridge Authority—to authority."

ALEX B.:
THE MAN COMPOSED ENTIRELY
OF *RECESSIVE GENES*

"I don't like it here."

"*Arthur, if you were doing undercover work for the CIA ,
you'd tell me... wouldn't you?*"

"In lieu of reading you your rights, we will have a moment of silence during which you may pray."

"*You will go to the hall closet. You will get your hat. You will get your purse. You will walk to your neighborhood grocer and you will take advantage of our special offer of three boxes of Sampson's Egg Noodles for the price you ordinarily pay for two. You will go to the hall closet...*"

"Call me at the office, we'll have lunch—you got my card."

"How can your country cite us for human rights violations when we are doing our utmost to reduce the number of political prisoners?"

"In this region, we still have a modicum of freedom."

"And I say unto you,
I'm O.K., you're O.K.!"

"Amen, brother!
You're O.K. and we're O.K.!"

"Victory. Peace. Two. All I know is it drives them bananas."

"Polly wants to parrot the party-line."

Do you love me?

Say you love me...

Sweetheart

I love you...

"*Can you explain why* your *papers are in order?*"

"I'd just like to know what in hell is happening, that's all! I'd like to know what in hell is happening! Do you know what in hell is happening?"

"Shhh, not here. Let's talk about that out in the corridor."

MCRAWFORD

"Now let's see what the Ministry of the Future has in store for you."

APEX
COMPUTER SYSTEMS

S. GROSS

"*We want you to know this is just a* preventive *execution.*"

"I say, 'It's overkill or be overkilled!'"

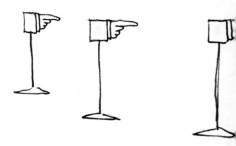

"Sooner or later, Larry, you're going to have to start trusting the government."

"He's charged with expressing contempt for data processing."

BOOTH

"It's no use, honey. If he's on the educational channel, he's on all the channels."

"Now here's a nice safe little investment. It's an 11% tax-free bond issue to finance the construction of clandestine prisons."

*"Now, should you decide to join our organization you will be
surrendering certain liberties."*

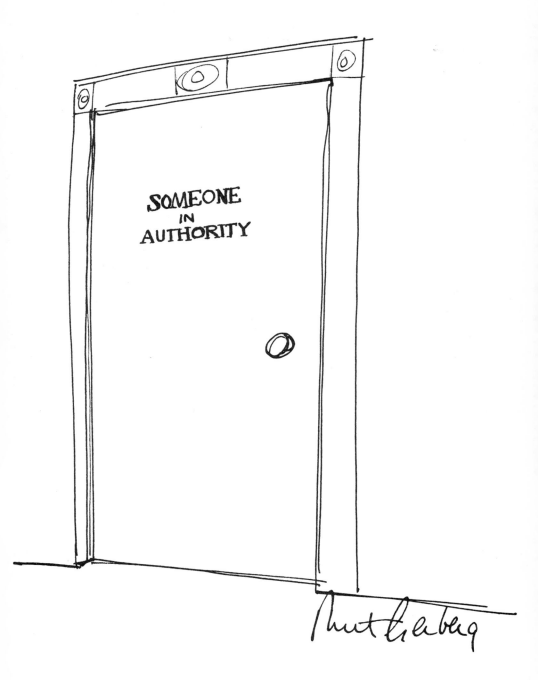

S.GROSS

"Watch it! You two have grumbled enough."

"Somehow, it's not how I had imagined it..."

"We have some facts about you that you don't remember, some facts about you that you thought were really secret, and some facts about you that never even happened."

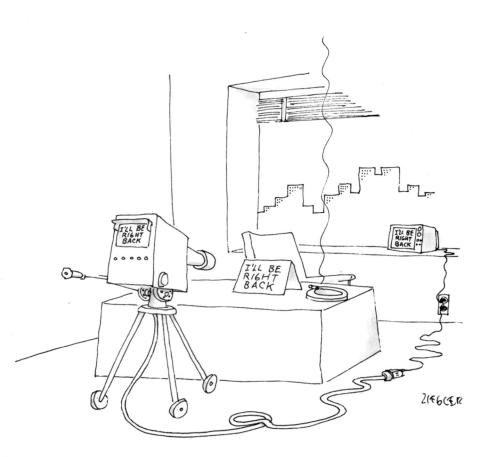

"Psst...I, for one, liked the book."

On the morning of January 27, Lawrence Emerson awoke to discover that he had become a mere fixture.

"I don't want to talk with him! Put him on 'destruct'!"

NOT TO CHANGE THE SUBJECT

"*The way I see it, once you start treating them as human beings, you've had it.*"

"In my opinion…"

S. GROSS

"Then he says to me, 'Lie down on the couch and tell me everything you are thinking!' Can you imagine!"

"Yup. This is dial-a-hitman. Who do you want vaporized?"

"O.K., now Reed, Bruno, Parker & Van Patten, Inc., followed
by Hanover, Norris, Upham, Wallace & Peck."

"I can't alk-tay ow-nay."

"He picks them up along the way.
They're people who follow like sheep."

"If someone had shown me the awesome face of justice years ago, I would never have become a dissident."

"That's nothing—I once imposed a 23-hour curfew."

S.GROSS

"I keep getting this feeling we're being watched."

"*See there! ... The System* does *work.*"

"Look, if you don't want to watch the movie you can sleep. But we can't have you reading."

"They say it's a battle for our minds."

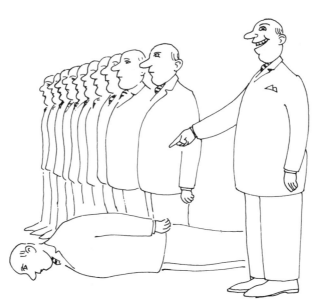

"Ha, ha, Bill fell down."

DONNELLY

Nov. 28 (UPI)–At his office in the capital city the world's most powerful dictator greets the world's funniest standup comic (Official Government photo).

"There are no great men, my boy—only great committees."

"Back to your roast in a minute, but first these directives from the Ministry of Food."

FUTURISTIC
STEREOTYPES

"Young man, in a hundred years no one's going to remember this...I sentence you to a hundred years...court adjourned."

"...notice how the eyes seem to follow you everywhere..."

"Maintaining confidence between the people and the government is extremely important...Lately, I, the government, have been losing confidence in you, the people."

"Quite frankly, we're as baffled by this current turn of events as, we're sure, all of you out there are."

"Now here's a bit of advice. Successful secret police keep their viewpoints middle of the road."

"Thank you for not smoking."

"The charges, your honor, are concealment of identity,
possession of a dangerous weapon, and we're waiting to hear
from the Bureau of Weights and Measures."

3.2

"...and so, to put it simply, heredity means that if both your mother and your father were born the third child in the family, you will be born the third child in the family."

"It was a televised press conference. The man from the state-controlled newspaper asked a searching question, the man from the state-controlled TV station asked a penetrating question, and I like a dope, asked a tricky question."

3·29

"*Take it from an old hand in the profession, son: Until you learn how to be cruel to yourself, you'll never really know how to be cruel to others.*"

Where Will It All End?

R. Chast

ELEMENTARY: THE CARTOONIST DID IT

Robert Mankoff

From one of *The New Yorker*'s most original and talented cartoonists! This is the only available collection of his amusing, dotty cartoons. Readers of *The New Yorker, Saturday Review* and *Rolling Stone* will immediately recognize Mankoff's unconventional, hilarious and bizarre wit. His unusual subject matter (ranging from liberalism to evolution and junk food), his particular brand of offbeat humor and his distinctive style make this an invaluable collection to countless Mankoff devotees.

"Robert Mankoff, as regular readers of *The New Yorker* know, is the Seurat of the cartoon world, an artist who builds his very funny panels with the precision of the great pointillist…a handsome Avon paperback original."

Los Angeles Herald-Examiner

75318-9…$4.95

PRATT INSTITUTE LIBRARY

This book due on the last date stamped below.
Fine of TEN CENTS per day thereafter.

DUE	DUE
JAN 17 1989	
MAY 20 1989	WWW
NOV 29 1998	
DEC 5 1998	FEB 12 1998
	WWW
DEC 5 1998 RECEIVED	MAR 2 1 1998
PRATT INSTITUTE LIBRARY	MAR 2 9 1999
OCT 1 0 1995	
OCT 2 9 1997	MAR 1 7 1999
MAR 1 7 1998	MAR 2 1 1998
NOV 1 1999	